THE FOREST

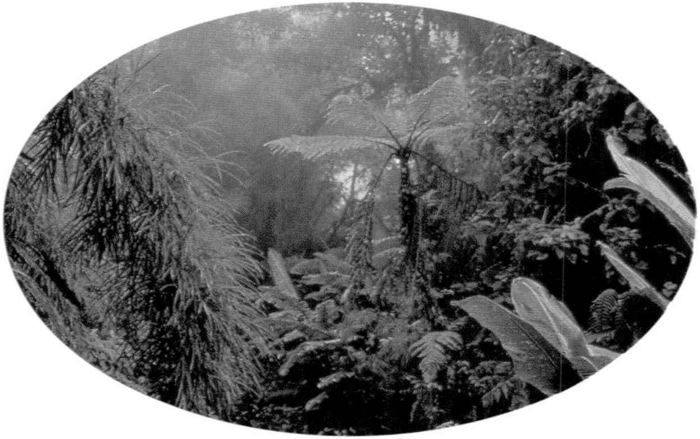

Kimberly Kern

Rigby

Here is a tree.

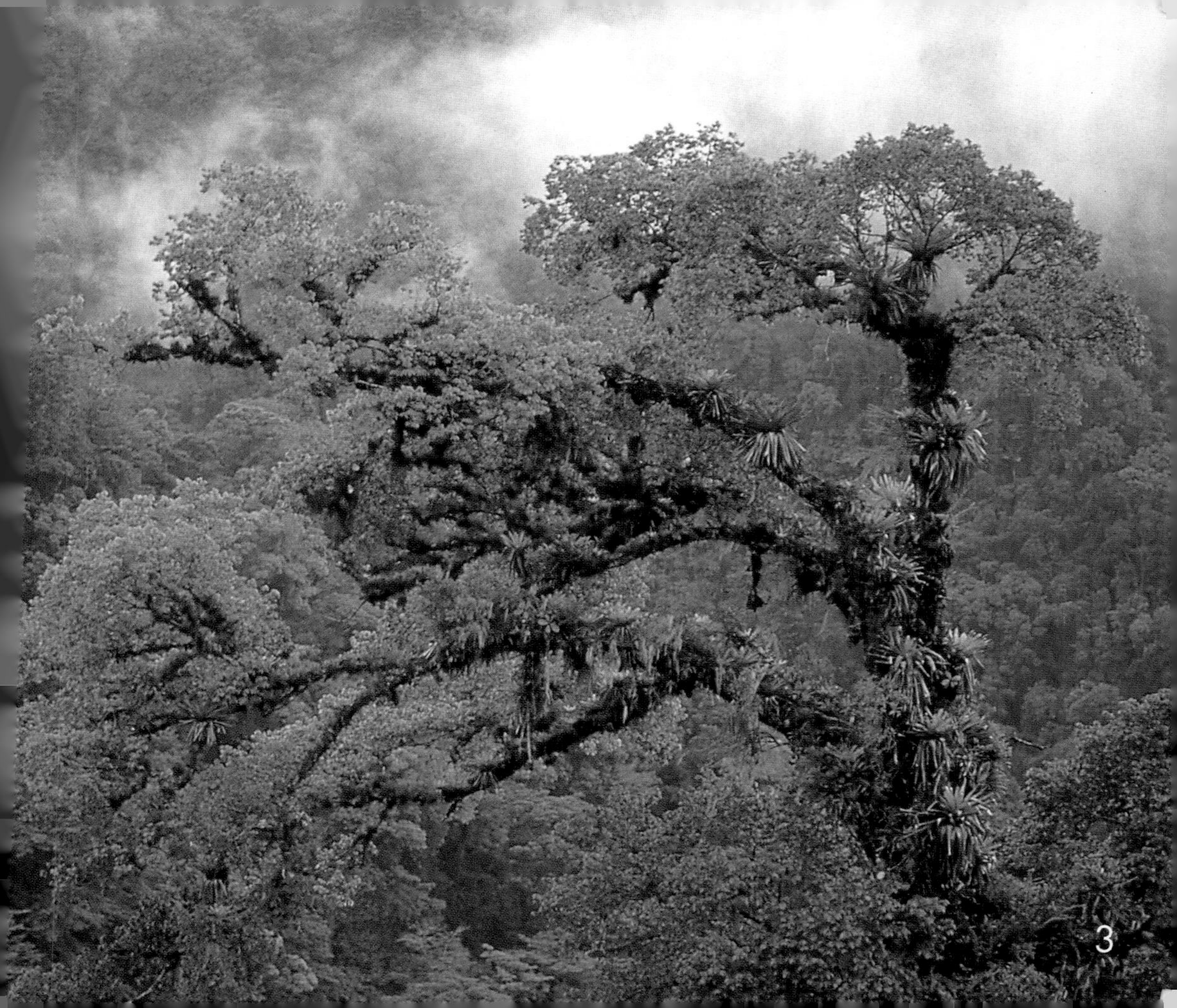

Here is a bird.

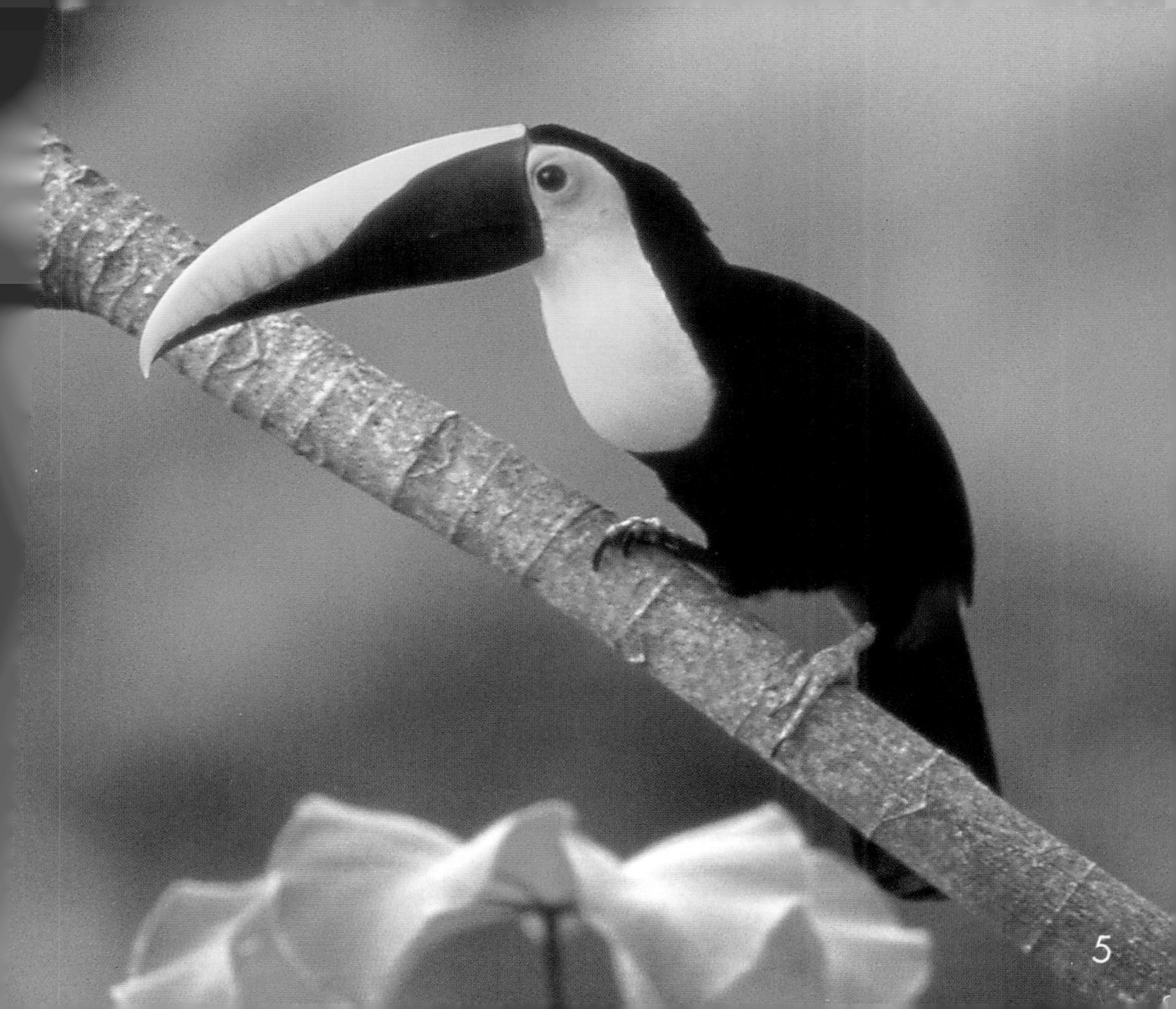

Here is a frog.

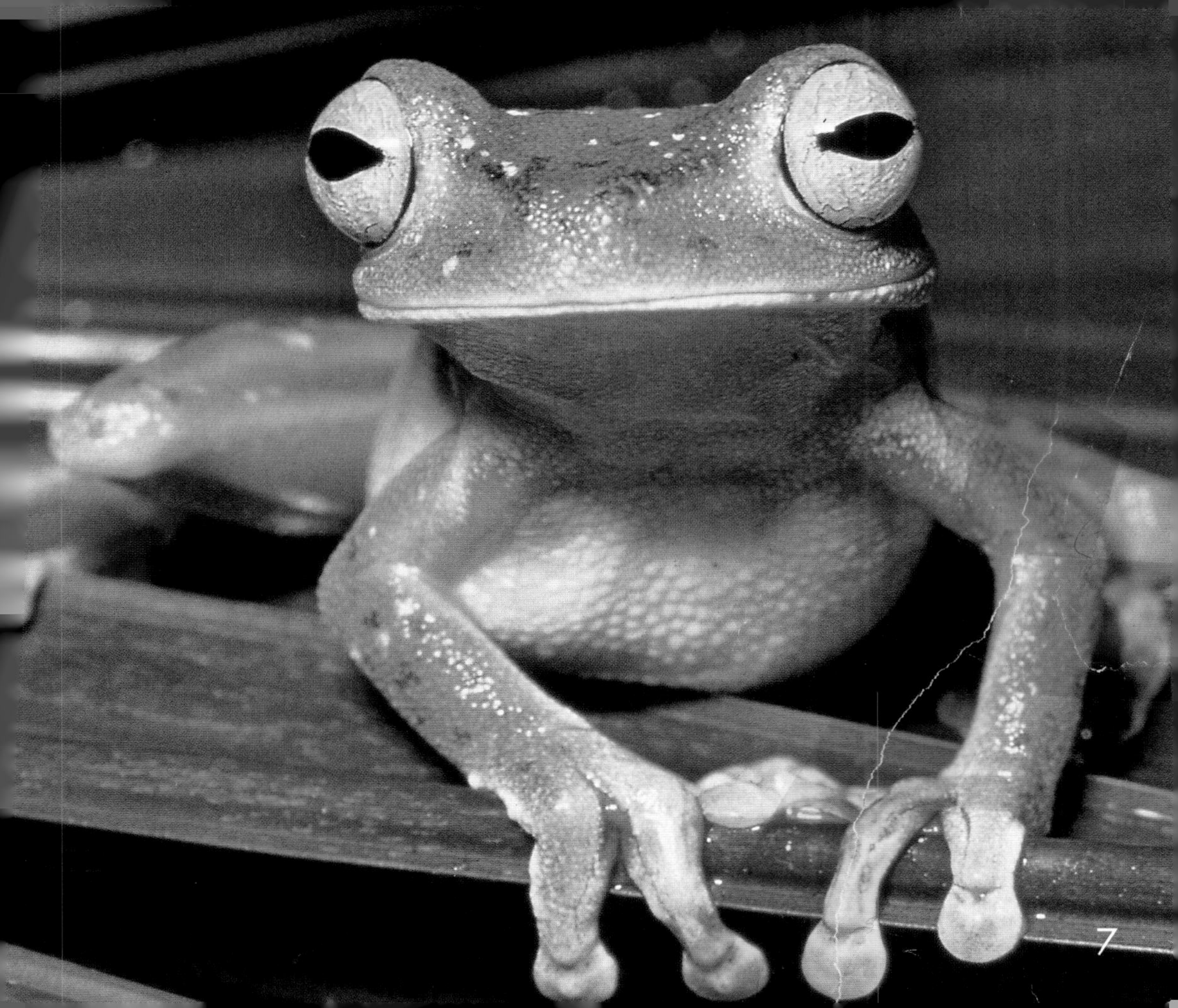

Here is a spider.

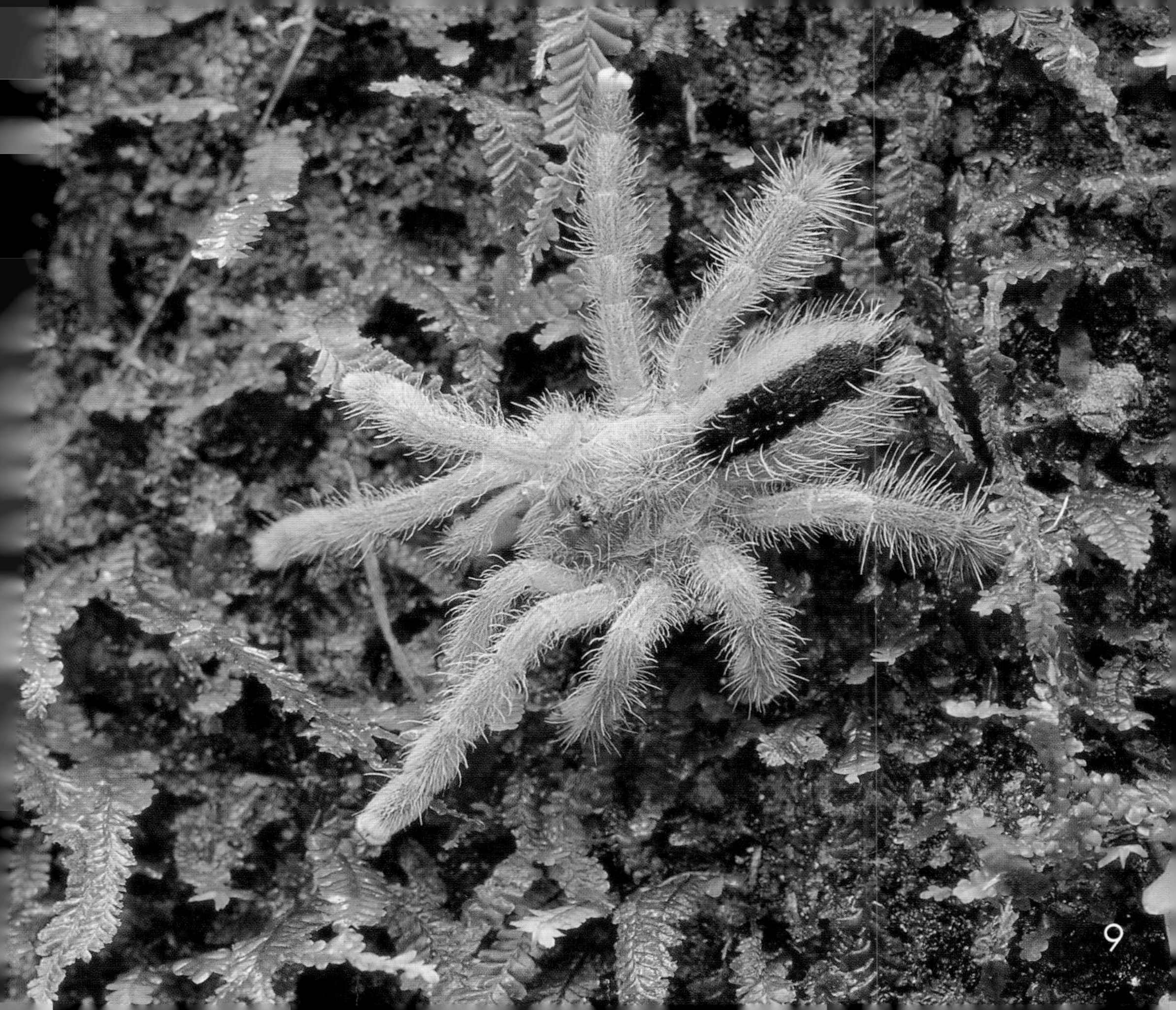

Here is a lizard.

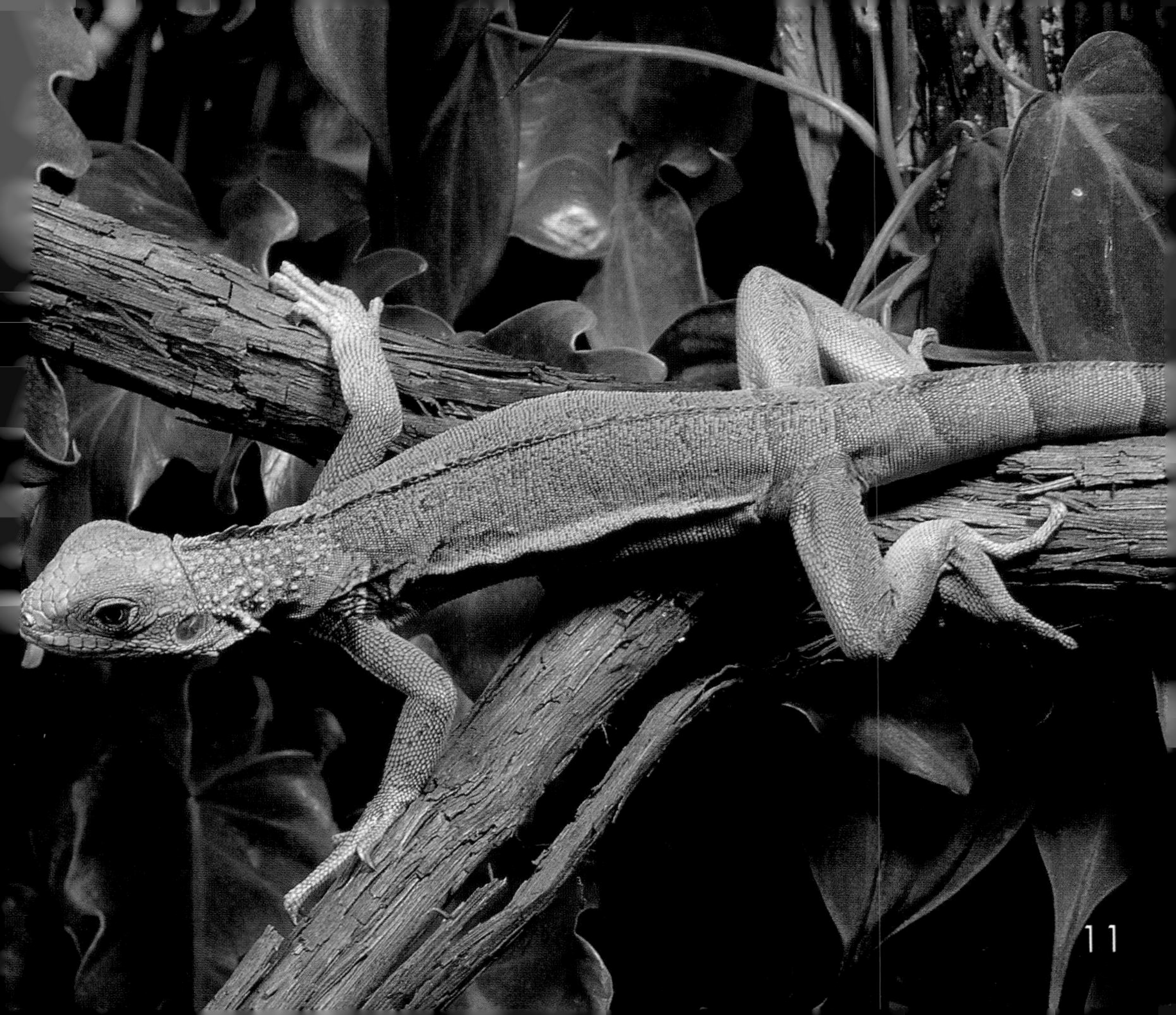

Here is a snake.

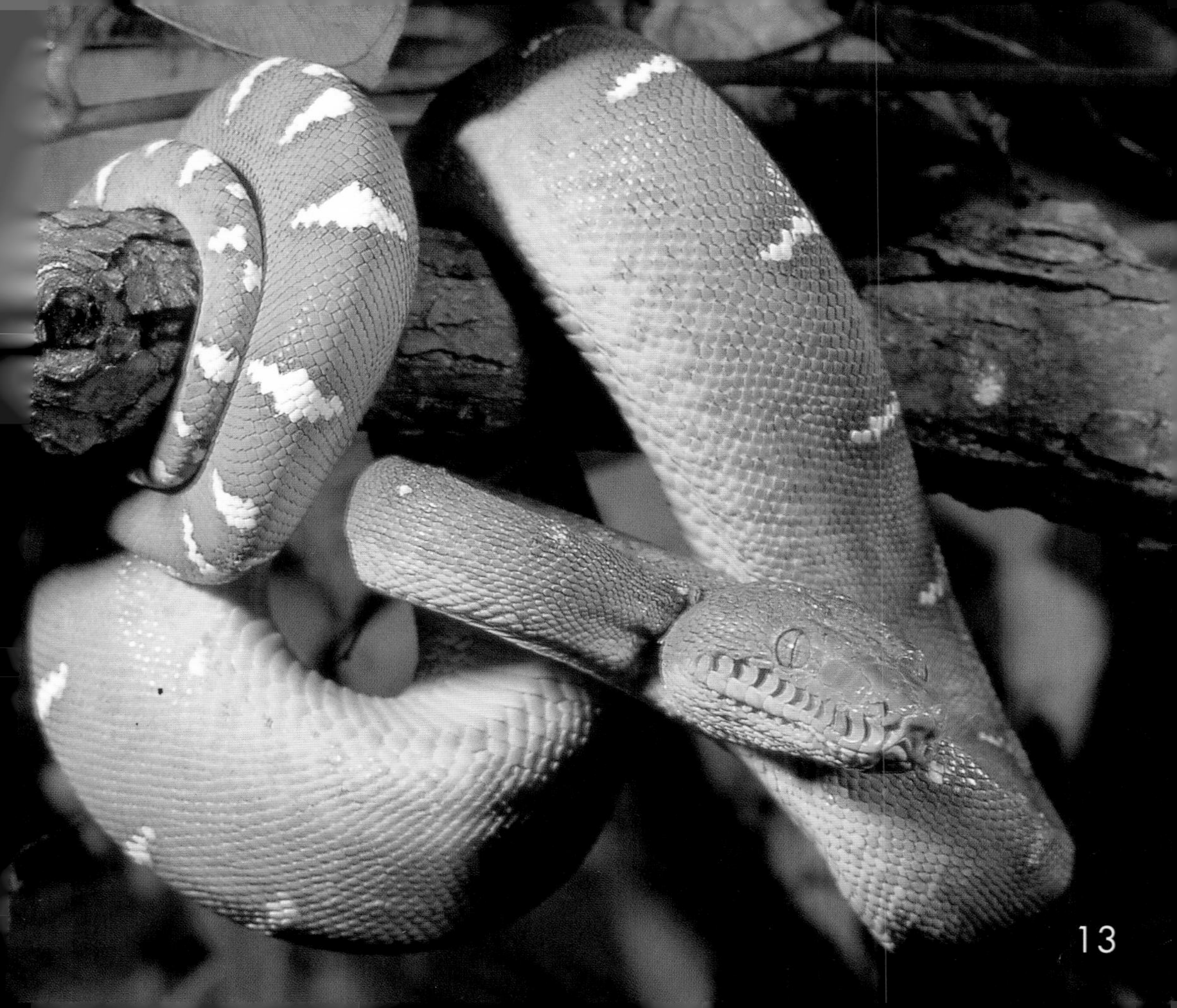

Here is a monkey.

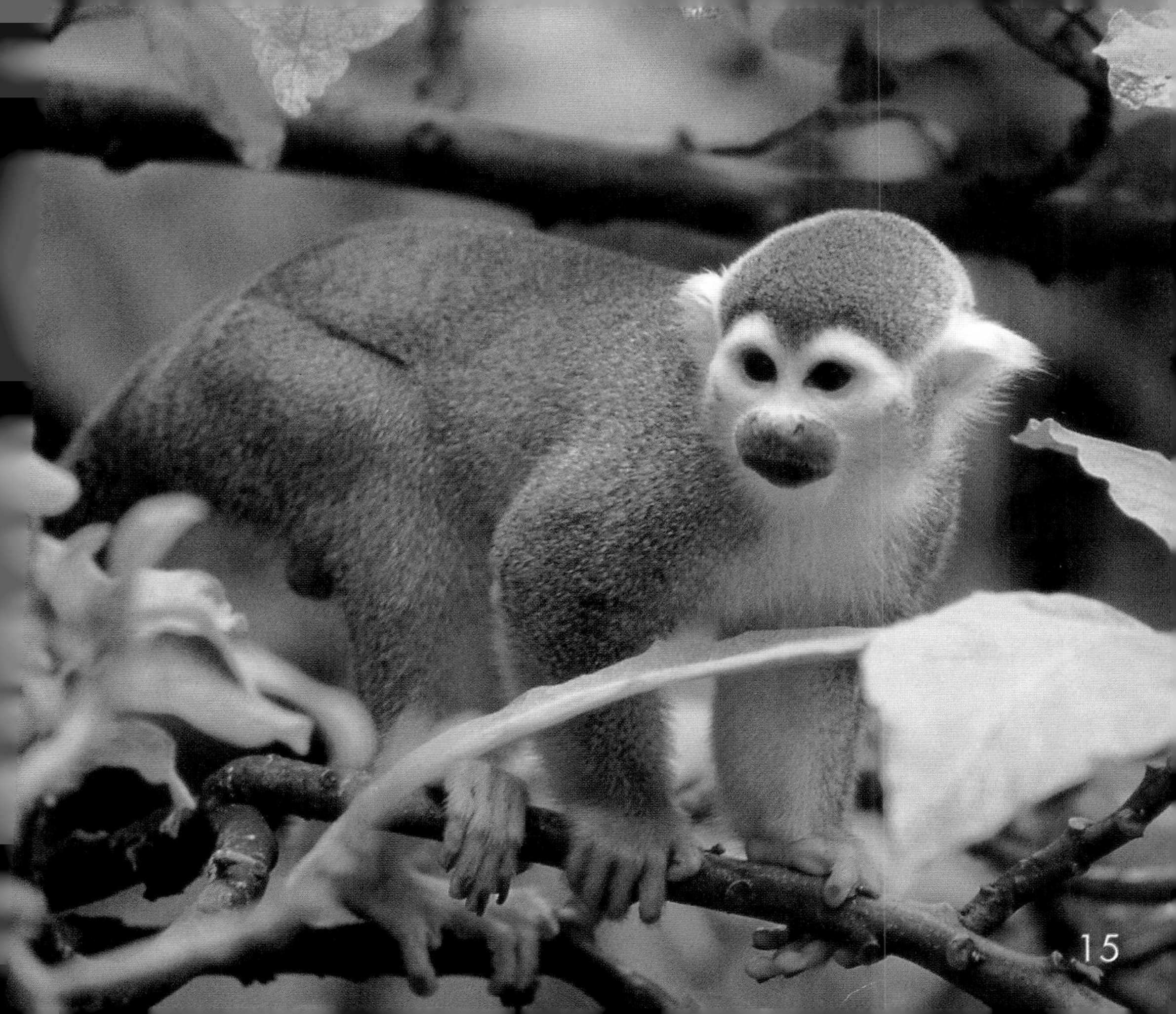

Here is a forest!

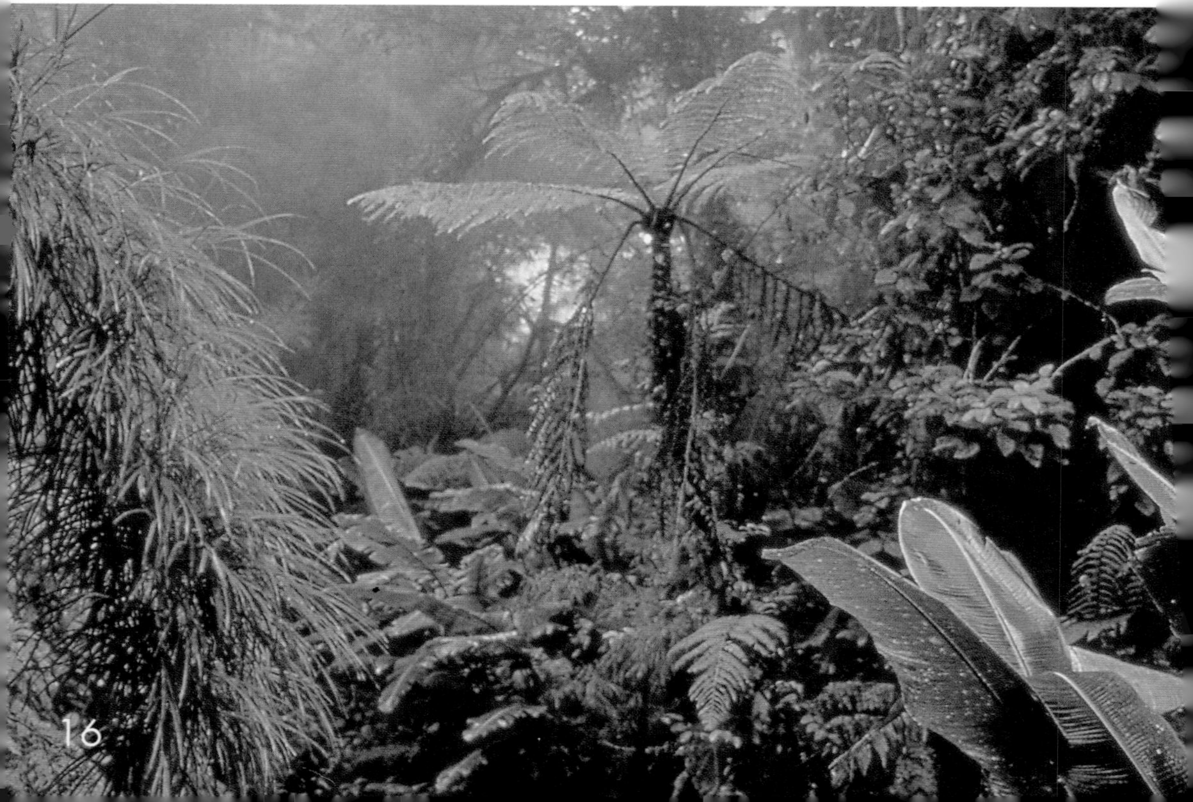